ROBERT DENKER

125 REASONS TO BE A NUDIST
– And A Few Reasons Why Not To Be One!

outskirtspress
DENVER, COLORADO

The opinions expressed in this manuscript are solely the opinions of the author and do not represent the opinions or thoughts of the publisher. The author has represented and warranted full ownership and/or legal right to publish all the materials in this book.

125 Reasons To Be A Nudist – And A Few Reasons Why Not To Be One!
All Rights Reserved.
Copyright © 2015 Robert Denker
v1.0

Cover Photo © 2015 thinkstockphotos.com. All rights reserved - used with permission.

This book may not be reproduced, transmitted, or stored in whole or in part by any means, including graphic, electronic, or mechanical without the express written consent of the publisher except in the case of brief quotations embodied in critical articles and reviews.

Outskirts Press, Inc.
http://www.outskirtspress.com

ISBN: 978-1-4787-5861-7

Outskirts Press and the "OP" logo are trademarks belonging to Outskirts Press, Inc.

PRINTED IN THE UNITED STATES OF AMERICA

Contents

Weddings 1

Workplace/School 6

Travel/Recreation 11

Family Situations 17

Politics 22

Commerce 26

Miscellaneous 31

How the world will have to be re-titled (Books, Songs, Movies, etc.) 35

If God intended people to be naked, they would be born that way.
- Oscar Wilde

Why write a book about nudism?

The world of nudism is often misunderstood by the textile world. The general population thinks of nudists as eccentrics and deviates, yet many nudists are prudish and, yes, even Republicans!

Your clothes conceal much of your beauty, yet they hide not the unbeautiful. And though you seek in garments the freedom of privacy, you may find in them a harness and a chain. Would that you could meet the sun and the wind with more of your body and less of your raiment.

Khalil Gibran, The Prophet

Weddings

1. Bridal Party not stuck with those ugly bridesmaids' outfits.
2. When the invitation says, "Black Tie Optional," that's exactly what it means.
3. You have two options to "dancing cheek to cheek."
4. You never have to worry about someone else wearing your outfit
5. Brides don't have to worry about anyone stepping on their train.
6. Best Man has options on how to carry the rings.
7. Bride can wear something borrowed and something nude!
8. Bachelor party can use the stripper money on more important things – booze!
9. You really know who the 'best' man is!!
10. It's so easy to slip off the bride's garter.

On the other hand.........

11. You better not have hot soup on the menu

12. You better be very, very careful when you cut the wedding cake

13. Boutonnière can be very painful

14. Groom may not want to dance with the mother-of-the bride

Indecency, vulgarity, obscenity - these are strictly confined to man; he invented them. Among the higher animals there is no trace of them. They hide nothing. They are not ashamed.

Mark Twain (Letters from the Earth)

Workplace/School

15. Everyday is "casual dress for workday."

16. You never ever have to hear, "Your fly is open."

17. Save a fortune on dry cleaning bills.

18. A nudist doesn't waste time in the morning deciding what to wear.

19. A nudist never puts his (her) clothes on backwards.

20. All school uniforms are standard.

21. You never get ink stains in your pocket.

22. You can't get caught for cheating in anatomy class.

23. Never have to match shoes to your outfit

24. No panty lines

25. Nudist students are always honest

26. Show and Tell and school will take on a nude meaning.

27. People will know if you did something half-assed backward.

28. You no longer can dress down an employee.

On the other hand.........

29. Everyone knows when you play the "it's that time of the month card" – that it's that time of the month.

30. You will have to be very, very careful in lab class.

31. You will have to avoid certain jobs, such as, Steam Presser, short order cook, pneumatic drill operator, etc.

We are ashamed of everything that is real about us; ashamed of ourselves, of our relatives, of our incomes, of our accents, of our opinions, of our experience, just as we are ashamed of our naked skins.

George Bernard Shaw

Travel/Recreation

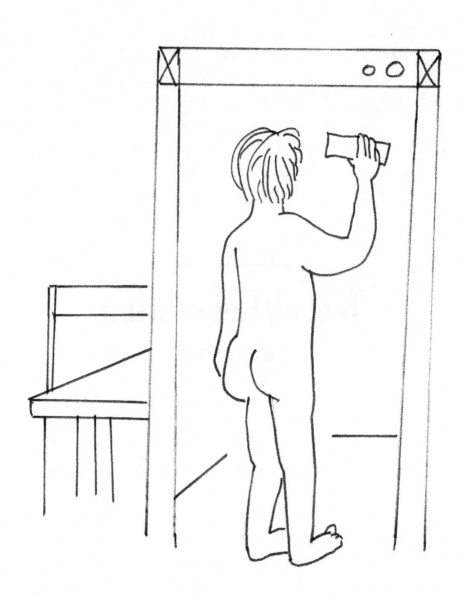

32. You can *fly* through airport security.

33. It discourages terrorism.

34. No long lines at the woman's rest rooms.

35. Only have to learn to ride bare back.

36. Movie will never be rated 'R' for nudity.

37. We can get rid of Joan Rivers asking, "Who are you wearing"

38. Playboy Centerfolds will be provocatively overdressed.

39. People will read Playboy for the articles.

40. We would no longer be subjected to those movies where the women's dress is always torn discreetly so that the only material left just happens to cover strategic areas.

41. Nor would we see those corny scenes where all you see is the woman's garment falling from a rear angle shot to indicate that she is undressed.

42. Finally we would not see those scenes where two people are engaged in hot and heavy doses of copulation only to be sure that they are snuggled under the sheets when the camera shoots down on them.

43. The musical Hair can be seen by the audience for which it was intended – teenagers.

44. Get that all over tan.

45. Don't have to bother with dress rehearsals.

46. Real men will be able to do three-handed pushups.

47. A study conducted by the West German Olympic swimming team concluded that even just wearing bathing suits slowed down the swimmers.

48. Men would have an advantage in a three-legged race.

On the other hand...

49. You will need a lot more sun tan lotion

Adam and Eve entered the world naked and unashamed - naked and pure-minded. And no descendant of theirs has ever entered it otherwise. All have entered it naked, unashamed, and clean in mind. They entered it modest. They had to acquire immodesty in the soiled mind, there was no other way to get it. ... The convention mis-called "modesty" has no standard, and cannot have one, because it is opposed to nature and reason and is therefore an artificiality and subject to anyone's whim - anyone's diseased caprice.

Mark Twain (Letters from the Earth)

Family Situations

50. You never have to hear, "does this dress make me look fat?"
51. You never have to worry how to dress the twins
52. Strangers never have to ask a nudist parent if the baby is a girl or a boy.
53. No protests over breastfeeding in public.
54. More closet space for everyone (So now you have a place to keep all of the junk you got for Christmas).
55. Nudists never waste money on push-up bras.
56. Children never outgrow their clothes
57. You never get ugly ties for Christmas
58. Cheating husbands have more time to jump out of the Motel windows!
59. Cheating husbands don't have to worry about lipstick on their collar
60. Children will not have to wait before they ask, "Where do babies come from?"
61. No more laundry sorting
62. No more ring around the collar
63. Children will play intern rather than doctor
64. Siblings & parents can multitask in the bathroom.
65. You never have to dress for dinner – even at IHOP!
66. Easy to put fever thermometer in one of two places
67. You would be allowed to wear maternity clothes to differentiate vs. those women who were just obese.
68. There will be a lot less morons asking, "Are they identical twins?"

On the other hand...

69. When you are sitting shiva (Jewish post funeral obligation), you will need several towels to cover the boxes

What spirit is so empty and blind, that it cannot recognize the fact that the foot is more noble than the shoe, and skin more beautiful that the garment with which it is clothed?

Michelangelo

Politics

70. You won't be attacked by PETA.

71. Nudist politicians have no one in their pockets.

72. We would be spared the arguments about whether or not Hillary should wear skirts or pants outfits.

73. All lies will be barefaced!

The body says what words cannot.

Martha Graham

Commerce

74. You will sell a lot more towels.

75. A new industry will be creating for inventing a way to hold your credit cards and cell phones.

76. Don't have to push closet space as a perk when renting an apartment

77. Hair dying will be a *two-step* process.

78. We can get rid of those ugly Clothes Bin Donation Centers.

79. Gynecologists will no longer insist that a woman wear a gown while he probes her genitals and makes her open it to examine her breasts.

80. Electrolysis commerce will be in boom times

81. No interview will contain that stupid question "Do you sleep in the nude?"

82. There would be a paper called the NY Daily Nudes.

83. Slippery nipples will take on a new meaning.

84. All clothing sales will be 100% off!

85. A clotheshorse will now refer to a shy equine.

86. Transsexuals can become more original.

87. Clothes are incubating grounds for bacteria and are often probably the main cause for yeast infections.

88. Coppertone would become a Fortune 500 Company.

89. Viagra would get a lot of free advertising.

90. Shoe salesmen would be able to multitask as GYN's.

91. Shoplifting would become very very difficult!

92. We would need a lot less Customs agents.

93. Stores could display more merchandise in the areas that had try-on rooms.

94. Doctors would be able to make freelance diagnosis just by riding on the subway.

95. Quickies would be Quickiers!

96. You never out grow your clothes and your clothes are always in fashion.

97. Nudists require less surveillance in deli marts.

98. Vogue, Elle, & Harpers would be the name of a Legal firm.

99. All automobiles will come standard with heated seats.

100. Benjamin Franklin was a nudist – and made it to the Hundred Dollar Bill

Men are even lazier than they are timorous, and what they fear most is the troubles with which any unconditional honesty and nudity would burden them.

Friedrich Nietzsche

Miscellaneous

101. Nudists don't need a vivid imagination.

102. Nudists can never cheat at poker.

103. Nudists always look you in the eye when you are talking.

104. Statistically nudists are less likely to engage in crimes of physical violence against women

105. Everyone can admire all of your tattoos and body piercing.

106. Don't have to worry which way the hospital gown goes on.

107. Studies have indicated that bras cause breast cancer.

108. Don't have to waste time rolling up your sleeve for flu shots.

109. No one will ever say, "your slip is showing."

110. No clothes chapping.

111. Don't have to look at men in Speedos.

112. No bra straps pinching or sticking out.

113. No shrinkage in the wash

114. Shoplifting will become a lost art, as will be pickpockets.

115. Men don't have to worry about shrinkage in the ocean

116. How Britney Spears and Lindsey Lohan get out of the car is unimportant.

117. We would be spared the jokes about who wears the pants in the family.

118. Don't have to worry about the last two drops rolling down your pants leg.

119. The word Peeping Tom will be removed from the language

120. Being tight-lipped will take on a new meaning.

121. You don't have to worry about your socks falling down

122. You don't have to worry about getting your tie in the sauce

123. No more wedgies!

124. You don't have to worry about your shirttail sticking out

125. If you don't like someone you can *sun* him or her!

How the world will have to be re-titled (Books, Songs, Movies, etc.)

1. No clothes maketh the man
2. The Nudist and the Dead by Norman Mailer
3. The Emperors no new nothing by Hans Christian Andersen
4. The Nude Lunch by William Burroughs
5. Liar liar nothing on Fire
6. Nude by David Sedaris
7. Nude in Death by J.D. Robb
8. The Nude Brothers Band
9. Bare Nude Ladies
10. The Nude Ape by Desmond Morris
11. The nude sun by Isaac Asimov
12. The nude Chef by Jamie Oliver
13. One nude baby by Maggie Smith
14. Nude Prey by John Sanford
15. Nude Boys Singing
16. The Nude Jungle with Charlton Heston
17. The Nude Gun
18. The Nude City TV Series
19. The Nude Spur with Jimmy Stewart
20. A stitch in time saves nothing!
21. The Nude Maja.

22. Itsy Bitsy Teen Weenie Yellow nothing

23. Undressed to Kill.

24. Lady in Skin Color

25. Undressed to the 9's (Sorry women - not what you were thinking about)

26. We could have a new TV show called Nippleodeon

Bob Denker has been a nudist for over 15 years. This book evolved out of an essay he wrote for Newsweek Magazine in 2007, entitled, "I'm Happiest in My Birthday Suit", in which he set forth the virtues of being a nudist.

He would like to thank Randy Lotowycz of Workman Publishing for encouraging him to write this book. He would also like to thank Amy Kassiola for her tasteful illustrations.

Special Thanks to Mary Miller

He would like to thank his family for accepting him as he is.

Finally he would like all of the crew at Gunnison Beach in Sandy Hook, New Jersey for giving him the reason to go on being a nudist.

Bob is married with two children and two grandchildren and currently lives in Staten Island, New York

CPSIA information can be obtained
at www.ICGtesting.com
Printed in the USA
BVOW08s0447200217
476595BV00001B/8/P